ISLANDERS

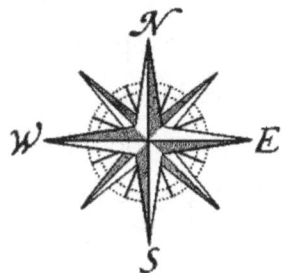

Stephen Brooke

Arachis Press 2023

Where do you travel, this fine day?
I but seek to find my way.

Islanders
©2023 Stephen Brooke and the Arachis Press

All rights reserved. The text, art and design of this publication are the copyrighted work of Stephen Brooke and the Arachis Press and may not be reproduced nor transmitted in any form without the express written permission of the author or publisher, other than short quotes for review purposes.

ISBN 978-1-937745-87-5

Arachis Press
4803 Peanut Road
Graceville, FL 32440
http://arachispress.com

ISLANDERS

Stuff

The best poems are about
stuff. Like love and death
and maybe wheelbarrows.
Painted whatever color you
fancy, of course. They'll
hold just as much stuff.

That poem about what happened
yesterday comes too late.
Tomorrow comes whispering
in timelessness, in Latin
and in French. It struts
across Elizabethan stages.

It has more stuff than you
could imagine, folded
neatly in its luggage or maybe
carted off in the wheelbarrow.
I think it is blue, this time,
but I have a spray can handy.

Hiding

Daylight runs into the sea,
hiding unless I call its name,
call across the breadth of this dark
sky. It always returns, holding
hands with the stars. They slip away,
those stars, but most return as well.
I have never needed to call them.

   a star falls ~
   my arms are too short
   to put it back

this compass
holds yesterday
as its true north

my ship sails
ever in circles

Islanders

From the sea of darkness, islands loom,
all along the street, each with its natives,
each with its own customs of the night.
Archipelagos of street lights rise
from rain-shiny asphalt; dim-lit diners
harbor sailors who have sought horizons
compass can not find. A moment's rest,
then sail on. A street must lead somewhere,
even in the night, and there are islands,
islands where the weary may find light.

   longing for home
   the sailor seeks known stars ~
   a million lights

a billion stars ~
can I choose only one
to make my wish?

Solitaire

I win, I lose
playing games of solitaire
through the night

does the next card
matter?

Roads

All the night I've driven, passed each ramp,
each with its whispered promise gone
among the headlights. Though I yearned to sleep,
I yearned more to find the dawn.
Count the markers to your destination—
unknown, it lies on maps not drawn.
Roads must end, whatever Tolkien said;
I can not go forever on.

    I pour myself one more dream.
    Will it be enough
    to fill me?

Valuable

Commodities. Valuable only
when someone is willing to pay
or to steal. You. Me.

Raped in the marketplace.
Sold into servitude.
How else know my worth?

How else know your worth
than to steal all that
is you? Take. Hold.

Toss aside, worthless.
Every coin changes hands.
Every coin becomes the game

of chance. Heads. Tails.
Life. Loss. I sit
unpurchased. Valueless.

The Counter-Puncher

It's the jab that sets it all up,
pop-pop, wait for the mistake.
Wait for that off-balance second
and you come in with a hook
to the ribs and a shoulder and clinch.

Counter-punch. Take his power
and whack him upside the head
with it. Life's a dirty fight, kid;
don't let 'em tell you otherwise
and don't be afraid to step on some toes.

Heart? Sure, you need heart
but all your fire won't stop
an ice-water punch. I've seen
a thousand losers with heart,
seen them go down and stay down.

Getting lucky has never
been a matter of luck.
Wait for the moment. Wait
like a lover for that goodnight kiss.
It will come for the counter-puncher.

Happy Meals

If only happiness came in paper
wrappers from McDonalds,
'Happy Meals' for our souls.
If only happiness was as easy
to find as the nearest drive-up
window with bags of hot
fast-food bliss and little
packages of ketchup.
But we never catch up, do we?
Happiness is the wild animal
our forebears pursued and speared
with the joy of their blood.
Roses on the snow,
roses on the snow—
we no longer hunt that beast,
no longer wait, hidden
where it wanders, where it feeds.
We buy empty bags
and go to bed hungry.
Hungry.

The Atheist's Son

The atheist's son believes
less than his father. He sees
the empty horizon, knows
it matters not which way

we walk. God is dead
but so is Man, and now
each marches in the other's
slow funeral procession.

Clouds gather over there
but some wind sweeps them away;
the atheist's son composes
hymns to nothingness.

    I've rattled my dice too long.
    Why do I so fear
    to cast them?

Code

We are who we seem but only
in part. Donning new masks

to send ourselves yet more
coded messages,

we hint of where we might
have been found, yesterday.

To you, I speak with head turned
away, mumbling, hoping,

fearing to speak of today
lest tomorrow overhear

and become jealous.
Let me sing; let me

become a voice on the wind,
seeking your hidden heart.

My Father's Business

I am both the Christ
and the soldier who nailed him
to a cross. I have struggled

to forgive myself
even as I struggled
for breath and cast lots

over a worn cloak.
What kindness of wine
can I offer, what sop?

I must attend the cruelty
of this, my blunt business,
trusting only that I

shall wake tomorrow
or on the third day
to a new world.

Words

What good are words that serve, compliant little
words going about their business with a smile

and a bow? Tonight they wait on me, stand waiting
as I sate myself, help me to my bed, leave

and laugh, for I have won nothing, done nothing.
Give me words that fight back. Give me words

that use my words against me, sparring, scarring,
words that knock me down. I'll go ten rounds

with such words. I'll get up off the canvas
and go again. That wasn't a ten-count. I'm good.

What good are words unless we struggle? What good
am I, if I only let them serve and smile and leave?

   I play on~
   a guitar with no strings
   can still be a drum

Travelers

Where do you travel, this fine day?
I but seek to find my way.

May I journey by your side?
As you wish; the road is wide.

Would you let me take your hand?
You may ask but not demand.

Then, if I kissed you, would you cry?
To find out you need but try.

Will you love me if I love you?
Only if you love me true.

And if false my love should be?
I would surely set you free.

But if I should beg your pardon?
Once betrayed, my heart must harden.

What if my pleas were filled with passion?
Oh, but that is all the fashion.

If I love you will you love me?
Your love must be as deep as the sea.

What must I give to prove my love?
Give yourself; it is enough.

    be mine and *you're sweet*
    candy hearts would tell of love
    when we were too shy

Bow

What bow has set me to this futile flight,
Has sent me arcing to your armored heart?
Dare I trace the journey of that dart
To some willful archer of the night,

Some jokester god who, laughing, took his aim
At a mark no man might penetrate,
Leaving me to curse both love and fate?
No, I will myself take all the blame

And know I was a fool, as are men all,
For we choose to fly and, spent, must fall.

Blocks

Work in progress:
building blocks stacked,
each an inch

closer to heaven.
We never finish
piling B atop A

and One on Three
before toppling each other's
unsteady towers.

Pet

Love is neither a dog nor a cat
but it must be fed. Then maybe
it will sit in your lap and allow
you to pet it, thinking it will stay.

Honor

Honor is but hubris, dressed up,
sinful pride in a uniform,
emptiness posed as purpose,
selfishness as virtue.

I have pretended before the mirror,
admired this illusion,
my illusion, entranced by ego,
enamored of an image.

It is in humility, the putting
aside of warrior ways,
of shame and of honor,
that we see the real.

The distorted reflection of desire
enslaves us to our will;
it holds no right, no wrong,
knows neither love nor light.

I shall have no honor, no vain
pride in this false idol,
this misshapen lump I fashioned;
I have seen it is not real.

For Fear

I will not love for fear I'd love too deeply
and in the depths of you might I then drown;
refusing any desperate hope of rescue,
I'd willingly let passion pull me down.

I will not love for fear I'd love too simply,
a fool who chooses without asking why,
and when abandoned, as I'd surely be,
left with no answers why love went awry.

I will not love for fear I'd love too little,
unworthy of the love I may be given;
a liar and a sinner, soon discovered,
and from your Paradise I would be driven.

I will not love for fear I'd love completely,
forgetting all I am, all I have been;
or is to lose, perhaps, to gain in love
and ever this the destiny of men?

I will not love for fear of love's unknowns,
the secret paths that lead me to your heart;
ways on which I can only wander, lost.
I will not love for fear; I'll live apart.

Let

Let my love come from the east,
from the home of rosy dawn;
let a thousand birds awaken,
raise their voices to announce her
as she fares on silken breezes,
as my true love comes to me.

Let my love be of the south
where the forests of the sun
rise in trackless tangled splendor
and the stealthy tiger glides;
from far lands of dappled shadow,
let my true love come to me.

Let my love be from the land
to the west, be from the golden
shores beyond the mountains where
sun seeks sleep in Ocean's depths.
Ere I too fall into slumber,
let my true love come to me.

Let my love come from a land
in the north where snow lies white,
mounded like the breasts of maidens.
As the urgent winter winds,
restless, ever driving on,
so my true love comes to me.

Music

Your music ever plays,
ever distant, haunting
the edges of my life,

the motif to which
my heart returns, again
and yet again. And, so

I am here. I rise
in counterpoint, darkness
to light, despair to faith,

passion to passion. Sing.
Sing and I shall be
consumed by our music.

Silence

I have too many words and none are right,
so I give you not verses, but myself
to do with as you will, to keep or toss
onto your scrap heap with the rest of once.

For all I say seems empty, meaningless;
perhaps it but reflects the man I am,
who has no worth beyond what you may give
to me and that which I may give to you

in the silence of belonging to each other.

Lantern

a candle
hollowed by flame ~
burning still

the heart becomes
a lantern

Mantis Dance

Our courtship moves in patterned steps,
a pantomime of passion,

the invitation to an embrace
I willingly accept.

We will dance this mantis dance
until you devour me.

Puzzle

I was an odd shape—another
piece of sky in a box.

But your shape fits my shape
and your blue matches mine.

We become one picture until
we return to the box.

I may be in love with you.
Will you help me make
up my mind?

    His memory fills her heart.
    Will there ever be
    room for me?

I did everything she asked.
What should I do now
she is gone?

    I kept aiming for your heart.
    Did I shoot myself
    in the foot?

I lay awake beside her.
Why did that damn clock
still read three?

One More Tree

My heart is one more tree
in the forest of you.

When it falls, will anyone
hear but me?

Leftovers

You have nibbled away bits of my heart,
oh, you women I've loved, taken
small bites and put it back.

Go ahead, taste if you will
but won't one of you clean the plate?
I've no room for leftovers.

   song birds
   spread their news
   at dawn

   ours may remain secret
   for a while

Squeaking

The honey-colored hamster went
round and round, the squeaking
of his wheel a soundtrack
for our play, our awkward
acting of the love scene
I had just written in my mind.

Who would bother to count
the revolutions? We all go
around, you know, and think
we have arrived somewhere,
with fresh newspapers to tell
us things have changed.

In the dark silence of after,
not noticing the wheel
had ceased to turn, we whispered
of fate and of love but I
knew that each cage is somewhere
in a larger cage.

I and the hamster accept this;
we have put the world
in a cage, where it can
do no harm. Inside
is outside and my wheel
still goes round and round.

You will, someday see
the wires around you. This
I have known all along.
I have laid awake too many
nights beside you, and heard
the squeaking start anew.

   The size of the universe
    is measured by the distance
    from me to you.

   Tonight, infinity
   fills one room.

We wished upon the same star.
Will I receive all
you asked for?

Subjects

I am king of the sky
and all the stars are my subjects.
All the nations of night
attend me.

Walk with me in my court,
stay beside me;
you shall be queen of all
this silent promenade.

You shall be queen of my sky
and of my heart.

   birds fall silent ~
   pulling up covers of rain
   the sun sleeps in

   I rise and prepare tea
   allowing you also to sleep

My Distant Love
a ghazal

With longing, I pen verses for my distant love,
the words that tell how I adore my distant love.

Across the separating night I sing to her;
I loved no other so before my distant love.

My words are but the messengers I send ahead;
to meet her kisses I implore my distant love.

Again, I'll hold her in the doorways of my arms;
then I, this Lad, will love the more my distant love.

One Candle

Let one candle burn tonight,
so I might hold you in my eyes
as well as in my arms.
Then, as I drift to sated slumber
the sight of you
may fill my dreams

Hidden

I have lied to the moon,
telling her I have no love,
none kept hidden away.

I have lied to myself,
pretending I knew your heart
when I knew not my own.

I have lied to you and fear
now to seek the truth
your heart has hidden from the moon.

Cinco de Mayo

margaritas ~
between sips you say
let's just be friends

we dance
on Cinco de Mayo

Terrorist

Love was terror, my heart
hiding itself in fear
while you hunted it

down the winding crazy
streets of an empty city.
I felt too strongly then.

I had no ready weapon
other than the suicide
of waking to the day

where you, true believer,
followed through the shadows.
I should have shot back.

The Latest

You're
not the
first to tell
me it is fate.
Just the latest to be disappointed.

Pit

Our love became
a bottomless pit.

I threw pieces of myself
in each day, each hour,

but could never begin
to fill your need.

Wounded

Our love was a wounded animal,
Seeking a place to die.

There were no darkened forest depths,
No den where it might hide;

Only the cruel sun of passion
In a sky of despair.

Feared

I feared her as much as I loved her,
counting my hours, hours
of freedom and of bondage.
To return, one must

run away. How far?
To the end of her soul,
to the starless voids
between our galaxies.

To the end of that branch
where twigs sway in the wind,
touching now and again.
I glimpsed a light between

the trembling leaves and wished
upon it for my death
or perhaps for hers.
One as good as the other—

all things come back in time
but not the same. Never
the same—that is what
I feared and what I loved.

My Sin

I am the wall built brick by brick around you;
I am the army raised up to surround you.
I am this net of spells cast to confound you,
illusions that will dazzle and astound you.

I leave you with no option but surrender;
I hold you fast, oppressor and defender,
become your lover, terrible and tender,
beneath such nameless skies my dreams engender.

I am the priest who hears your each confession;
I am the penance paid for each transgression.
I am your darkest secret and obsession,
the whispered lie, unspoken indiscretion.

I sell myself to buy you as my slave,
condemning all that I would hope to save.
Fall on the altar laid within your nave;
I take away more than you ever gave.

I am where you shall be and you have been,
I am where you shall end and must begin.
I am the game you can not play to win,
For only I absolve you of my sin.

I Choose

You must be practical and so we part;
you'll ever follow your head and I, my heart.
Oh, yes, I knew all of this from the start
but cared not, for I chose to fall in love.

What you chose I now wonder; can you turn
emotions on and off, while I must burn,
repeat all my mistakes and never learn?
If I must choose, I choose to fall in love.

Rooms

You gave love by the room
when I desired houses.
Such small spaces; how could I
dwell there, ever a guest,

ever a visitor? I would not
have mussed your towels too much
nor broken all your china.
No, rooms were not enough;

my heart needed houses.

Resurrection

In the fading of my faith,
I ask how you became my church,
the true religion of my heart.

The hurt of you was all I had,
all I could hold close, believing
in your return, our resurrection.

I've not renounced this priesthood, no,
not yet; I'll watch the failing flame
of each candle lit to you.

I'll watch them fade, one by one,
and only then shall I turn from
your darkened altar, resurrected,

for all beginnings need an end.

   rain spoke through the night
   interrupting my slumber
   just as you once would

Empty

Her names are Love and Loss and my dreams
become empty. She breathed her way
into the night, once, a ghost
of memory and of imagination,
of past and future. Empty, I can not
find her song beside me.

   since the time you left
   the easel has stood empty ~
   I no longer paint

   only your portrait remains
   to remind me of those days

cool reflected light
filled the shadows of your face
erasing sorrow

I remember you so
sleeping beneath the trees

Victims

I had convinced myself I cared
but she knew better. We are always
the first victims of our seductions.
How else could we carry on?

For her, I counted the stars. Did she
believe my tally? I did; every
time, I did, even though
it never came out quite the same.

In the dark, her breathing told
me lies. If only I could sleep
they might come true. The ceiling
mocked me as I turned again.

Victims of the moon and stars,
and of each other, we shall make
believe as long as necessary.
How else could we carry on?

Swallowed

I would have swallowed you whole,
made your heart my heart,
your life mine, so none
could know our start or end.

Might we have been Ouroboros,
devouring ourselves eternally,
or simply disappeared,
consumed, both?

I have emptied my belly
of you, now, emptied
myself of your heart,
my heart, your life, mine.

> my road curves ahead
> leading away from you ~
> each step a goodbye

Trying to be
the man you thought me to be
I became no one.

Prayer

She was my litany, her name
The only prayer my heart would speak;
The only heaven I could seek
Lay in her power to reclaim
This soul.

What toll
Is paid the ferryman to cross
His water, once more join the living?
In water lies the great forgiving,
The baptism to wash all dross
Away.

Why stay
Among these shades? They grow more dim,
More empty with each torment they
Inflict upon themselves. I pray,
I sing, to Love in hopeful hymn:
Deliver me,

Deliver me
From yesterday.

Whisper

a memory
sleeps at my side
each night

I whisper your name
expecting no answer

The Last Time I Was Happy

What do I do now?
Write more of those sad songs?
I have too many, you know,
far too many already.
I've been singing them—
singing ever since
the last time I was happy.

    I have fallen down
    the stairs that led from you ~
    no graceful exit

Who I Am

Being who I am,

there are duplicates
of every love letter
I wrote you, organized

by date, in a box
with your name.
Yours are in there, too,

our words, interspersed—
you and I, between the sheets
once again.

Being who I am,

I keep my memories
on a closet shelf,
knickknacks I cannot

bring myself to discard,
revisited each time
I clean house.

Carefully, carefully,
I must return you
to your box, being

who I am.

Arms

last night
I made believe
I held you

my arms are empty
today

> two frauds conspire
> to believe each other
> for a while

What does one say
when there's nothing left to say
but goodbye?

The Dead

Bring out your dead:
and I come forth to lay
myself in his wagon.
Bring out your dead,

bring out your dead:
Each cathedral bell
joins the requiem:
massed voices clamor

Requiem aeternam
dona eis, Domine.
Where shall I lay my head
now but on earth's pillow?

The time has come and gone
and will not come again:
dies irae, dies illa.
I have brought out my dead.

Forests

I stumble along these pathways
  finding only darkness.

Trees rise to block my way
  where none grew before.

The forests of yesterday
  are filled with your night.

Offerings

How many candles should have burned
at the altar of our love?
I said a prayer with each I lit
until the air was thick with them
and the smoke. I spoke in tongues
of poetry; gibberish,
pretense and puffery, you scoffed
before you blew out my last flame.

Seven are the sacraments
I carry, three to the paper bag
and a baptism still wet in my hair.
I baked the bread myself; the wine
came for Winn-Dixie. In sharing them,
become my last rites, my anointing
into another life. I give
you the loss and glory of wind,

in the fullness of time a spring sky.
A procession passes, singing
Lamb of God. I hold the moon
to my face and see the wolf
within. Our good shepherd is out
searching and left you here with me.
Shall we light two more tapers
in memory of who we were?

    our bridges are burnt
    but I may still wave to you
    across the abyss

Elephant Man

I, too, am this man,
this monster, this mask within
a mask. Look away.

I, too, have hidden my face,
knowing its ugliness,
knowing the pain of truth

is akin to the pain of lies.
Why choose when each seems
as real as the other?

Know me by these, my rough
masks. The elephant man
can never bare his face.

    torn in pieces
    I am confetti
    for your parade

Fulcrum

I have teetered on the chair of your
words with rope chafing its reminder
along my tightened jaw. What good is holding
balance another breath? What point is there

in all this strength? Ah, to swing free of life!

Swing high, swing low, come for to carry
me beyond the river, carry me off the edge
of tomorrow. I've looked over Jordan
once or twice, or is it Styx? No matter;

the other side is darker than starless night.

I'll not find my way across like this,
poised on the unsteady fulcrum of desire
and of death. I wait, teetering,
teetering, for you to carry me home.

> I told you I didn't care.
> Why must you believe
> all my lies?

Visitors

Megrim and Melancholia,
siblings of the dark,
visit on the waning wind,
the sun a fading spark
in the ashes of the sky,
heaven's sullen arc.
Clouds lie close on my horizons;
despair is standing stark.

Drum of heartbeats in my head,
crashing, clanging gong;
light moves in a grotesque dance,
every rhythm wrong.
My guests crouch close on either side,
howl a hollow song
of loss and wordless yearning,
the yammer of the throng.

Curtains drawn about the world,
close around my pain;
forgotten wrong I can't atone,
loss I must regain.
Only imps and demons answer
prayers I whisper in vain;
brother and sister of the dark
come on winds that wane.

Singularity

The black hole at the center
of my galaxy
pulls in tomorrow, pulls
in the light of every
promised dawn. I spiral
inward, countless stars
drawn cascading in
my wake, all meaning, all
being, following.
It can not be seen.
It can not be named.
It but abides; it is.
The black hole swallows me.

Wounds

My rhymes are built of painful memory,
These scabs I pick to bleed anew each day,
These sores to which my fingers ever stray;
No one but I inflicts such wounds on me.

To offer some small proof that I still live,
In hollow evidence my losses stand;
Nor shall they while I, willing, wear their brand
Allow me to forget and to forgive.

Too long, in greedy need, I've held your name
As instrument to my slow suicide—
This dagger that once you may have supplied
I've wielded since and I must bare the blame.

Again, I open wounds so I might feel:
Each of these wounds I won't permit to heal.

> I was drunk with love for her.
> How much longer this
> hangover?

Starve

Your love is not enough—
dreams are my daily bread.
You fill me with yourself;
you quench my deepest thirsts

and yet, in time, I starve.
Starve as a drunkard does
who craves only his bottle.
Starve as the junkie, wasting,

forgetful of desire
that can sustain a life,
of appetite, of lust
for heaven's very stars.

Your love is not enough—
tomorrow I would hunger.

    I am not the man I was.
    Am I he you wished
    me to be?

The Act

I stepped forward,
holding my heart,
for your amusement,
for your applause.

The night laughs
as I try to sleep.

Pond

memories ~
stones cast into a still pond
banishing peace

the ripples spread and fade
until all is calm again

an image returns
one sitting alone
reflected

one broken string
will not be noticed ~
I play on

    I sought to buy happiness.
    Why did the price keep
    going up?

We were a pair of dreamers.
Why did she wake up
before me?

    lovers pass ~
    I remember your hand
    in mine

ropes of stars
strung across the heavens
hold night together

Leak

Today, the hole in me
is a slow leak.

I await the hour
when nothing is left.

Cup your hands for me
as I seep out.

Interesting

One
of us
stopped being
interesting.
I hope it
wasn't
me.

This Box

This little box of darkness was mine.
It was all I had, all I kept
for myself. I could not give you
that empty place.

Were you not the sun of my day?
You did not need my box of night
but you filled it with yourself
like a gift.

And what now shall I do with this
little box that was mine, this box
long hidden? I dare not lift the lid,
lest I lose you

and own, once more, a box of darkness.

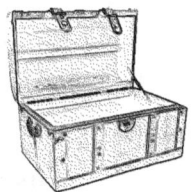

Hell

I have been an aristocrat
of emptiness, my sterile realm
of skewed sarcasm, poisoned perspective.

Better to rule in Hell? Thank you,
no. I'd gladly scrub the floors
of Heaven clean of every stain

trodden in by weary angels.

Wind
a sijo

The wind teaches the tree its song,
   whispering to each bud in springtime.

Falling leaves dance to its tune again
   when autumn bears them away.

Only empty branches sway now to its music
   as the winter wind sings of my loss.

A Good Thing

This is a good thing;
no, really it is.
Now my horizons
sing to me.
Now you are free
of my necessity.

This is a good thing
and tomorrow
will tell you all
I could not,
every story
whose ending I forgot.

Look into any mirror;
it is a sky
where our reflections
must take wing.
Kiss me and know
that this is a good thing.

Next Time

Next time we fall in love,
why not with each other?
It would make everything
so much simpler.

    I've never ghosted
    anyone but myself ~
    where did I go?

Vow

I abide
in a monastery
of the heart

my vow kept
by silence

Weep

If I cry, then I shall cry
as a hero, as Achilles
mourned Patroclus at the brooding
Trojan walls. Weep honestly,

openly, and then be done.
Who forbids my grief? No god—
they are made of human tears,
tears we set upon their journey

to the heavens. Only men,
only fools, deny their tears,
hoard them in their grasping hearts,
fear to set them free. Tomorrow

comes; the sun shall rise anew
for each man who wept today.

    I let my heart tell me lies.
    Is it time I stopped
    believing?

In Common

We never carried through
on that marriage thing,
never had to weigh
the transmuted metals

of our being against
each other. What have we now
in common save the fallen
leaves of another season,

time passed and not returned?
Better to grow apart,
apart, remembering
it was not always so.

>We're ships that pass in the night.
>If we collided
>would we sink?

Altar

The altar is stripped, the vestments folded
and put away. Your chalice has
been shrouded, housed in gold, to await
our sacrament. Shall I be priest

again? Shall I speak once again
to heaven? All that is made flesh
seeks consecration, yearns to join
as one. A moment—we know god

one moment and the moment slips
into eternity. The altar
is bare, the nave grown dark, and you
are now a statue, standing in shadow.

>   I entered you completely.
>   Can I ever find
>   me again?

Forgiven

All is forgiven if we can
but forgive ourselves. What we
bind on earth is bound in heaven.

So it is for each of us,
burdened by those things we will
not cast aside. Carry them

no further; all will be forgiven.

Dive

If the money's right, I'll take
a dive in the second round.
Let me look good for three minutes.
Let the crowd remember how I used to be,
who I used to be. It's not much.
It's all I have now, that and the envelope
you leave in the locker room.

Forge

I have held a destiny
forged in the smithies
of the heart, written
our love in hammer
and smoke and sinew.
I have bent myself double
with the labor. I have
burnt myself hollow.

So I've tempered fate;
so I've dreamed a future
to dance upon my hearths.
And all the while
you grow like a rose
from the hand of God.

    Your dreams were never my dreams.
    Why then do they still
    fill my nights?

Slip

I am the many things you remember
  but none of them is me.

I am the shadow the fallen tree
  once cast when you were young.

All these will slip from your fingers
  and flow away as the years.

    footprints tell me
    one has walked here before
    was it I?

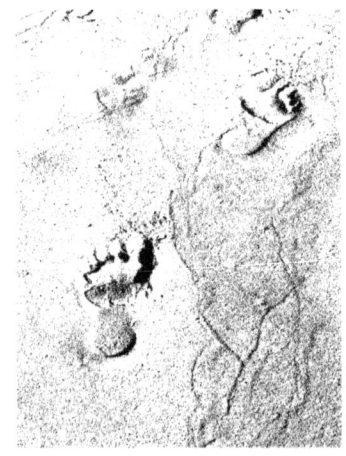

Cyclops

Polyphemus, old and blind, remembers
all that No One did to him in sunny
Sicily, where once he roved, a carefree
shepherd. Now his world is as darkened
as the cave he made his home, his wooly
flocks about him. He hears yet their voices;
their scent rises yet around, all mingled
with the salty tang of seas that tumble
on the shores of youth. Did No One voyage
far upon those waters? He heard only
voices calling, oars in fading rhythm,
passing into someone else's story.

> We two,
> wounded, longing,
> perfect for each other—
> that winter, we should have fallen
> in love.

Rope

God is the elephant and we
the blind men, understanding
in part but never comprehending
the whole. What part do I hold?

It doesn't matter. It is still
a part of God, even if it feels
like a piece of rope.

Actor
a sijo

Like any good actor
  I truly live my parts.

You can believe every word
  when I say I love you.

Remember I may someday
  be cast in other roles.

Taller

Trees were taller then, and days longer.
Even the sky was further away, the clouds
distant as the memories that floated
off into that endless echoed blue.

Night knew whip-poor-will and owl and stars
rising from the hemlock-shrouded ridges,
rising from the hidden hollows where
darkness slept; but I slept too, and dreams

found their way to me. Days were longer,
trees were taller, and I understood
nothing, lost among them. Let me glimpse
green horizons, hills now half-remembered,

once again and learn what journey carried
me to shores I never once had dreamt.

    not all answers
    come to those who ask questions
    listen to the wind

Horizon

The sky stretches above, the earth
exists below. The mind creates
the line between. It is a line
we can not reach. We know that.

Yet we yearn to cross, to touch
that elusive illusion and know
what lies on the other side
of nothing. Which horizon calls

today? Only the one I created.

www.ingramcontent.com/pod-product-compliance
Lightning Source LLC
Chambersburg PA
CBHW020021050426
42450CB00005B/588